Sell your books at
World of Books!
Go to sellbackyourBook.com
and get an instant price quote.
We even pay the shipping - see
what your old books are worth
today!

DISCOVERING THE UNITED STATES

Texas

BY MARY SHAW

Kids Core

An Imprint of Abdo Publishing
abdobooks.com

abdobooks.com

Published by Abdo Publishing, a division of ABDO, PO Box 398166, Minneapolis, Minnesota 55439. Copyright © 2025 by Abdo Consulting Group, Inc. International copyrights reserved in all countries. No part of this book may be reproduced in any form without written permission from the publisher. Kids Core™ is a trademark and logo of Abdo Publishing.

Printed in the United States of America, North Mankato, Minnesota.
052024
092024

THIS BOOK CONTAINS RECYCLED MATERIALS

Cover Photo: S. W. Cargill/iStockphoto
Interior Photos: History and Art Collection/Alamy, 4–5; Steve Byland/Shutterstock Images, 7 (top left); Shutterstock Images, 7 (top right), 20–21, 22, 28 (top right); Brian Luke/Shutterstock Images, 7 (bottom left); Matt Jeppson/Shutterstock Images, 7 (bottom right); Photography by Deb Snelson/Moment/Getty Images, 8; Elizabeth W. Kearley/Moment/Getty Images, 10; Operation 2022/Alamy, 12–13; T. Lesia/Shutterstock Images, 14; Everett Collection Historical/Alamy, 15; Brett Coomer/Houston Chronicle/Hearst Newspapers/Getty Images, 16; Leena Robinson/Shutterstock Images, 18, 24; NPS Photo/Alamy, 23; Endeavor Moore Photography/Shutterstock Images, 26, 28 (bottom); Red Line Editorial, 28 (top left), 29

Editor: Laura Stickney
Series Designer: Katharine Hale

Library of Congress Control Number: 2023949372

Publisher's Cataloging-in-Publication Data

Names: Shaw, Mary, author.
Title: Texas / by Mary Shaw
Description: Minneapolis, Minnesota: Abdo Publishing, 2025 | Series: Discovering the United States | Includes online resources and index.
Identifiers: ISBN 9781098294144 (lib. bdg.) | ISBN 9798384913412 (ebook)
Subjects: LCSH: U.S. states--Juvenile literature. | Texas--History--Juvenile literature. | Southwestern States--Juvenile literature. | Physical geography--United States--Juvenile literature.
Classification: DDC 973--dc23

All population data taken from:
"Estimates of Population by Sex, Race, and Hispanic Origin: April 1, 2020 to July 1, 2022." *US Census Bureau, Population Division*, June 2023, census.gov.

CONTENTS

CHAPTER 1
The First Juneteenth 4

CHAPTER 2
The People of Texas 12

CHAPTER 3
Places in Texas 20

State Map 28
Glossary 30
Online Resources 31
Learn More 31
Index 32
About the Author 32

Early Juneteenth celebrations featured music and dance performances.

CHAPTER 1

The First Juneteenth

It was 1865. Since 1861, northern and southern US states had been fighting in the American Civil War. One thing they fought over was slavery. Many Black people were enslaved in the South. They were forced to do difficult work for no pay.

People in northern states wanted to outlaw slavery. But people in southern states disagreed. They wanted to keep slavery.

In 1863, President Abraham Lincoln freed enslaved people in most southern states. Texas was the southernmost state, so news took longer to reach it. Many Black people in the South did not know they had been freed. On June 19, 1865, Major General Gordon Granger came to Galveston, Texas. He announced that enslaved people there had been free since 1863. People celebrated the news. In 1866, they held the first Juneteenth celebration. Families gathered for cookouts, fireworks, and parades.

Today, Juneteenth is celebrated across the country. In 2021, Juneteenth became a

Texas Facts

DATE OF STATEHOOD
December 29, 1845

CAPITAL
Austin

POPULATION
30,029,572

AREA
268,596 square miles
(695,660 sq km)

STATE BIRD

Northern mockingbird

STATE TREE

Pecan

STATE FLOWER

Bluebonnet

STATE REPTILE

Horned lizard

Each US state has a different population, size, and capital city. States also have state symbols.

federal holiday. Every year on June 19, people in the United States gather and celebrate freedom for all.

Cacti such as prickly pears grow in dry desert areas throughout Texas.

Land and Wildlife

Texas is in the US region known as the South. Arkansas and Louisiana border the state to the east. To the north is Oklahoma. New Mexico borders Texas to the west. South of Texas is Mexico. The Gulf of Mexico lies to the southeast.

Texas is the second-largest US state by area. Forests, mountains, prairies, and deserts cover it. The state's highest point is Guadalupe Peak. It is 8,751 feet (2,667 m) tall. The state has many rivers too. These include the Rio Grande, Colorado, and Brazos Rivers.

Texas is also home to many animals. These include armadillos and rattlesnakes.

Bridge Bats

Austin, Texas, has the largest urban bat population in the world. Each year, more than 100,000 people visit Austin to see the bats. At **dusk**, people watch the bats fly out from the Congress Avenue Bridge for their nightly meals.

Armadillos live throughout Texas. They have armor-like skin and use their claws to dig for food.

Texas longhorn cattle live on the state's plains. But not all animals in Texas live in natural areas. About 1.5 million Brazilian free-tailed bats live under the Congress Avenue Bridge in Austin, Texas.

Climate

Different parts of Texas experience different weather. Sometimes tornadoes strike northern Texas. Hurricanes can hit the southeastern part of the state. The Rio Grande Valley in southern Texas has mild winters. The panhandle in northern Texas may experience blizzards. The Gulf Coast has a mild, moist climate because it is near the ocean. Areas farther inland are drier and hotter.

Explore Online

Visit the website below. Does it give any new information about Juneteenth that wasn't in Chapter One?

Celebrating Juneteenth

abdocorelibrary.com/discovering-texas

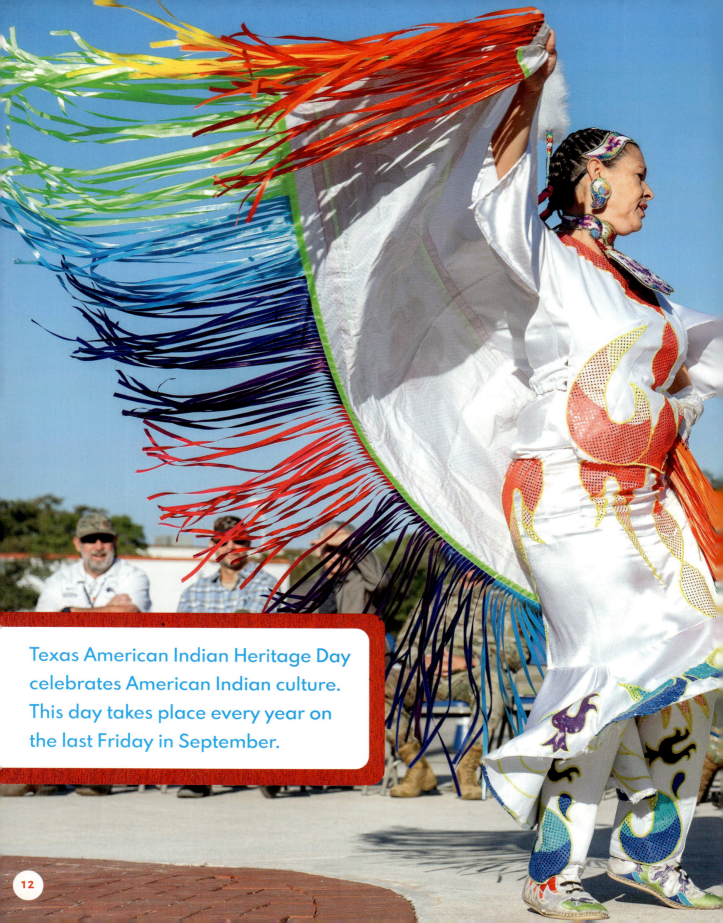

Texas American Indian Heritage Day celebrates American Indian culture. This day takes place every year on the last Friday in September.

CHAPTER 2

The People of Texas

American Indian nations have lived in Texas as far back as 37,000 years ago. These nations include the Apache, Comanche (Nʉmʉnʉʉ), and Wichita peoples. The Apache and Comanche hunted bison. The Wichita grew corn, squash, and beans.

Texas's state flag is known as the Lone Star Flag. It has red, white, and blue colors.

Immigration

Spanish **missionaries** settled in Texas in the 1600s. Settlers from southern states came in the 1800s. Many of these settlers brought enslaved Black people to work on farms. By 1860, more than 180,000 Black people lived in Texas.

Many Mexicans lived in Texas before it was a state. They were called Tejanos. Other Mexican **immigrants** came to Texas in the early 1900s.

President Lyndon B. Johnson lived on a ranch near Johnson City, Texas. The LBJ Ranch is now part of a National Historical Park.

In 2022, 40 percent of Texans were white. Forty percent were Hispanic or Latino, and 13 percent were Black. Six percent were Asian, and 1 percent were American Indian. Today, there are three federally recognized American Indian tribes in Texas.

Several US presidents come from Texas. Lyndon B. Johnson was born there. Presidents George H. W. Bush and George W. Bush have also lived in the state.

In rodeos, people compete in events such as barrel racing, saddle bronc riding, and tie-down roping. Tie-down roping involves using a rope to catch a calf.

Culture

Food is a big part of Texas's culture. Tex-Mex is a popular American **cuisine**. It features Tejano dishes with a Texan twist. Chili con carne is one

Tex-Mex dish. This spicy soup contains meat and beans.

Texas is also known for its cowboy culture. The official state sport is rodeo. Rodeos are contests. Cowboys test their riding and cattle managing skills. Many Texans wear cowboy hats and boots.

Other sports are popular in Texas too. The state has many major professional sports teams. One is the Houston Astros, a baseball team.

Chili Queens

The Chili Queens were a group of women in the late 1800s and early 1900s. They served chili con carne at outdoor food stands in San Antonio. Some people say the Chili Queens made Tex-Mex cuisine popular.

Farmers in Texas raise many breeds of cattle, including longhorn cattle. In 1995, the longhorn was named the state large mammal of Texas.

Industry

Texans often say everything is bigger in Texas. One major industry in the state is farming. Texas has the most farms and cattle of any US state. Farmers grow crops such as cotton.

Other Texans work in the energy industry. Texas is the country's biggest producer of oil and natural gas. The state is known for generating wind energy. It has many **wind turbines**.

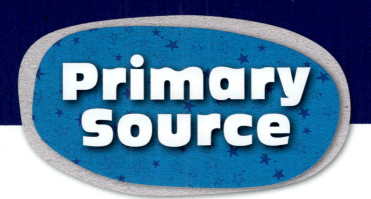

Texan David Henderson is a cattle rancher. He spoke about raising cattle:

> When you're growing something that you know somebody's going to be happy to eat, it's satisfaction that . . . you're doing something right and somebody's happy with what you're growing.

Source: Charlsie McKay. "Nurturing a Legacy." *RFD-TV*, 24 Apr. 2023, rfdtv.com. Accessed 11 Dec. 2023.

What's the Big Idea?

What is this quote's main idea? Explain how the main idea is supported by details.

The Colorado River flows through downtown Austin. A dam on the river creates two lakes in the city, Lake Austin and Lady Bird Lake.

Places in Texas

The capital of Texas is Austin. It is in central Texas. The city is known for its music and arts community. Houston is in eastern Texas. It is the state's most populous city.

Corpus Christi and Galveston are located on the coast. El Paso borders Mexico and New Mexico.

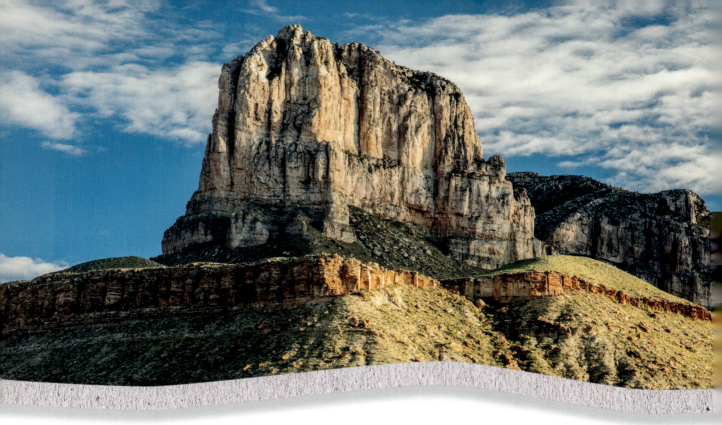

Guadalupe Mountains National Park is home to some of the highest mountain peaks in Texas. One is called El Capitan.

San Antonio has many historical sites. Dallas is home to the Dallas Cowboys, one of the state's major professional football teams.

Parks

Texas has two national parks in the Chihuahuan Desert. One is called Big Bend National Park.

Kemp's ridley sea turtles nest along Padre Island National Seashore. In the summer, thousands of people gather to watch the hatchlings crawl into the sea.

Cacti grow there. Animals such as round-tailed horned lizards thrive in the park's dry climate. At Guadalupe Mountains National Park, people can see mountains made of **fossilized** coral reefs.

At Big **Thicket** National Preserve, kayakers can paddle through a **bayou**. The preserve is home to unique plants that eat bugs. Padre Island is a National Seashore. In summer, visitors can watch sea turtle eggs hatch.

Big Tex wears a giant shirt and jeans made from real fabric. The statue also has a recorded voice that says "Howdy, folks!" to people at the fair.

Landmarks

Each year, more than 2 million people visit the State Fair of Texas. It has the most visitors of any US state fair. Visitors go on rides and eat fried foods. One famous sight at the fair is Big Tex. This statue is the world's tallest cowboy. He stands 55 feet (17 m) tall.

Houston is home to Space Center Houston. Visitors can see exhibits about the first moon landing. They can learn about space travel too.

The Alamo and San Antonio missions are historic landmarks in San Antonio. They mark the site of an 1836 battle. Visitors can learn about the history of these buildings.

The First Moon Landing

On July 20, 1969, the *Apollo 11* spacecraft landed on the moon. The team at NASA Mission Control Center directed the astronauts. Visitors can see the control room and *Apollo 11* rocket at Space Center Houston.

The Alamo is also known as the Mission San Antonio de Valero. It was built in the 1700s. Throughout its history, the Alamo has been used as a church and a military base.

From big Juneteenth celebrations to big bowls of chili, most people find that everything really is bigger in Texas! People can hike in the state's mountains. They can visit rodeos. Or they can explore historical sites such as the Alamo. Texas is full of big adventures for everyone.

Further Evidence

Visit the website below. Does it give any new information about the Alamo that wasn't mentioned in Chapter Three?

Battle of the Alamo

abdocorelibrary.com/discovering-texas

State Map

KEY
- Capital
- Park
- City or town
- Point of interest

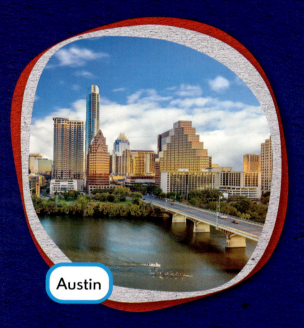
Austin

The Alamo

Glossary

bayou
a slow-moving body of water

cuisine
a style of cooking

dusk
when the sky starts to turn dark in the evening

fossilized
preserved from a very long time ago, such as imprints in stone

immigrants
people who move to a different country

missionaries
people who travel to other lands to spread their religion

thicket
a dense group of trees

wind turbines
large machines that change wind energy into electrical energy

Online Resources

To learn more about Texas, visit our free resource websites below.

Visit **abdocorelibrary.com** or scan this QR code for free Common Core resources for teachers and students, including vetted activities, multimedia, and booklinks, for deeper subject comprehension.

Visit **abdobooklinks.com** or scan this QR code for free additional online weblinks for further learning. These links are routinely monitored and updated to provide the most current information available.

Learn More

Alexander, Heather. *Only in Texas.* Wide Eyed Editions, 2023.

Norwood, Arlisha. *The History of Juneteenth.* Rockridge, 2022.

Index

Alamo, 25, 27
American Civil War, 5–6
Apache people, 13
Austin, 7, 9, 10, 21

Big Bend National Park, 22–23
Big Thicket National Preserve, 23

Comanche people, 13

Galveston, 6, 21
Guadalupe Mountains National Park, 23

Henderson, David, 19
Houston, 17, 21, 25

immigrants, 14
industries, 18–19

Johnson, Lyndon B., 15
Juneteenth, 6–7, 11, 27

Padre Island, 23

sports, 17
State Fair of Texas, 24–25

Wichita people, 13

About the Author

Mary Shaw was born in Dallas, Texas. She is an editor, designer, and writer of children's books.